a torre **error**

POEMS

Kraftgriots

Also in the series (POETRY)

a torrent of terror

POEMS

rome aboh

kraftgriots

Published by
Kraft Books Limited
6A Polytechnic Road, Sango, Ibadan
Box 22084, University of Ibadan Post Office
Ibadan, Oyo State, Nigeria
℡ + 234 (0) 803 348 2474, + 234 (0) 805 129 1191
E-mail: kraftbooks@yahoo.com
www.kraftbookslimited.com

First published 2014

ISBN 978–978–918–207–7

= KRAFTGRIOTS =
(A literary imprint of Kraft Books Limited)

First printing, October 2014

Dedication

For Rowan; your father, Nathan Suhr-Sytsma, is a good man.

&

Odey's friend, my dad, you left me at the middle of the road...

Acknowledgements

... no true painter labours alone

ance breeds nothing but "vexed" verse. In our *community of practice*, we paint with words. This is exactly what I try to do here. The collection of poems, *a torrent of terror*, being a potent and poignant comment on the political quandary that has enveloped our community, can be read from diverse perspectives, but with one ultimate, unifying purpose: to feel, see and partake in the suffering meted on us by those we call our own people. My brush forays into the hearts of the masses, and paints down their everyday groaning in not just comprehensible language, but also in a way that re-presents their sufferings to them in a graphic style. The brush strokes (poems) are not all about providing a huge mileage of the moral emptiness and degradation that has enveloped society in more ways than one; they are also about providing myriads of alternatives. One of the alternatives to electoral promises, for example, which are shoved aside sooner than the politicians get into offices, is offered in the poem, "If again..."

But, such a poetic initiative is not without its troubles. It is fraught with danger within the contest between painters and the sources of hegemonic dominance. Could it be that I am not well aware of this? Well, the poem, "Righter" depicts that.

a torrent of terror is not all about painting sociopolitical illnesses, but acute emphasis is placed on love; the need to love and be loved, an ultimate definition of the human morphology. It is the explicit articulation of the human desire for belongingness, emotional identification and attachment that makes me to quickly remember you, M. T. Lamidi, my teacher, a core academic; you said to me that these brush strokes are lovely despite some *torrents of terror*. The metaphor of my existence can be traced to the personification of your humility and sincerity. And you, Godwin Ukwu, you have shown me that the antonym of hate is love; wickedness, kindness; mindlessness, mindfulness.

Some people are just planted along our path to boost our energy; and so, I appreciate you: Sarah Ukwu, Toja Okoh, Mary Specht, Chuka-Fred Ononye, Amaka Ezeife–secret witnesses and enthusiasts of my brush strokes; and Funke Oni, you said to me to follow my passion.

The last section of the collection, "Reflections," which traverses my political viewpoints, serves as a moral mirror which I deploy to reflect on the tendrils of my life; how others' lives have shaped mine in more ways than one. And you, my former students at the University of Ibadan and those at Dominican Institute Samonda, are my intimate friends and great teachers.

Every time I ruminate on the healing strength of painting or poetry, Patrick Akande flutters through the memory of my brush – a medical doctor, who understands the "medicine of literature". The painter does not live by painting alone, but also by the bread that flows from Rebecca Umaye Adie's kind kitchen. You, too, Benyin Akomaye Akande, the imagery of Uyo is unutterably incomplete without the alliterative notes from the dishes of your kitchen. We call you Aunty; your husband, our father, Joe Ushie, calls you Iye, but you are actually a mother as your door is opened to all: Greek or Jew – thank you, Mrs Joe Ushie for all tales words cannot tell.

You never got tired of reading, editing and proffering substantial suggestions which have made these strokes of brush a better collection of poems: Ifeyinwa Okolo and Nathan Suhr-Sytsma. Thank you, my friend, Charles

Akinsete, for reminding me of the power that rests in the strokes of adjectives.

At times or most of the time, the image to be painted lives in our memory, but we need the physical paint and brush to put the image on canvas: thank you for making this painting a possibility – Foresight Schools, Four Corners Ikom, Cross River State.

Foreword

Reminiscent of Maya Angelou's 'Why does a caged bird sing?'
rome aboh throws his verses in *a torrent of terror* like
charmed incantations with the prophetic proclamation: 'I
write verse,' because 'I'm vexed.' This 'vexed' ink is not just
because of the birth of 'ill-omened *politricksters*' but the very
fact of the human condition he finds himself and the ills that
humanity masochistically invokes on self: 'all I care is/to
write about bitter memories/of hunger-swollen-belly kids'
and 'mine-ridden streets of Khartoum.' Like the oracular
beads of the diviner's *ipeh*, the book is divided into three parts:
patriotism, patterns of love and reflections; while the titles
of the poems read like podcasts of charmed amulets like,
'writer' as 'righter', *'ible'* and 'hour of truth', etc.

Geographically, the poems in this volume traverse diverse
climes: Tehran, Pyongyang, Darfur, Bamako, Guantanamo
Bay; and, Japan, Britain, Gaza and Harare–or wherever there
is human oppression or signs of it–not forgetting the Bakassi
people whose 'umbilical cords [are] uprooted and dumped
at The Hague.' 'a letter to the mp' reminds one of a recent
NTA news report of undernourished children in one northern
state of oil-rich Nigeria, as though the country is back to
civil war years when it was common sight to see 'kwashiorkor
and mumps' and 'eczema-coated skin'; against the noise and
pomp of our 'Sinators' who 'use the masses like a menstrual
cloth.' The poet seems to be warning Nigerians and the so-
called democratic world to beware who they vote for.

The poem 'the blind lead the sighted' speaks of our country
and the likes of us in 'the real Bermuda Triangle' where the
'blind lead the sighted'; where 'riches sit on wretches' in a
'Ghana-must-go-democracy'; where the love of the nation is
in 'their swelling Swiss accounts'; while we 'yawn of haunting

hunger' in a nation of 'dark days' where the 'maze becomes a weapon.' The poet asks: 'should we go to Endor…?' Then 'the evidence from Okija' springs up in 'maniacal pomposity': 'it's do or die' with the new-fangled 'democratized vocabulary'- '7-Point Agenda, Vision 20:20:20, Reformation Agenda,' amidst long queues for fuel. 'i see' speaks of Assad in his Syrian Hums, and Aleppo and Damascus with 'human flesh flying over plutonium-infested-homes'; and like in Nigeria where we are, like Buridan's Ass, caught between 'ass kicking *militeria*' and 'honey-coated-tongue *politheifians*.' 'Aljazeera' captures the violence-filled contemporary media whose stock in trade seems to be increasing the global divides between religions: 'the crescent and the star' and 'the cross'; in the same way they fan embers of passion between the East and the West. Today popular politics and governance have become synonymous with journeys on roads that take us away from 'the real roads' that will lead us to desirable ends. The universities which are supposed to be centres of learning and development also become victims of this *sukugo* or *wanderjahre* culture. From this complication arises the idea of 'federal character' which legitimates the enthronement of mediocrity in the name of national equity.

The poet turns to matters of the heart and away from social ills in the second section of the book. 'labour of love' reveals the 'love-sick minstrel,' a popular thematic phenomena among artists and poets who smart with overflowing emotions for love perpetually kept in abeyance. The poet persona suffers this as a result of cross-racial relationships which naturally bleach out colour barriers and bridge geographical difference and distance. The persona accepts this experience as it truly defines the real 'contours and substance of my existence.' The flip side of this sublime experience is the beloved's infidelity within treasured relationships. Nevertheless, the possibilities of love are not diminished; as captured in the closeness of images in 'allegiance.' He 'hugs [himself] in the warm thoughts of you' –when love is absent or kept in abeyance as it often happens because of the 'dollar sign.'

In the third section 'reflections' the poet persona waxes philosophical as he turns his gaze inwards away from the 'vexations' of the physical environment, with an ode to 'Time,' which records, recollects, and reflects every bit of life. These reflections are stylistically short, pithy and epigrammatic. 'i am ... I' sounds like some Bette-Bendi diviner's chant but which, though of the new age, unfortunately gets linked back to the Greek Apollonian prophetess and mistress to Agamemnon, Cassandra. Here, the poet persona bewails his particular 'hard luck' for he 'tills rocks for yam mounds.' This same persona is that 'brown dusty-footed infant/ wending the winding way/to the farms at *Akorgiagba*.' The space again changes to the ever-haunting academic scape of Ibadan University in 'candle in the dark,' and this archetypal metonymic professor, who 'brew his students like good wines.'

In a similar manner of homage, 'dad, and dads' is an ode to our 'scolding and cuddling fathers.' 'dad, and dads' remembers the fathers' who '... emptying [their] salary/into your extravagant pockets;/impressing in our hearts/we owe the same to our generation'; this is antithetically paralleled with our contemporary 'lethargic age' where these same children from good caring parents 'do nothing, [but] expecting everything.' However, one wonders from the perspective of our multi-cultural post-coloniality, why Dad's altruistic, exemplary paths should have led the child only to Jesus, and not anywhere else! And for balance comes 'forgettin', dedicated to Mama who is 'like poetry written/by the fireside during harmattan.' The mother becomes for the poet persona, 'the prime professor ... scholar one, professor emeritus, home teacher,' concluding with a whine: 'Oh my

11

sweet loving mama!'

Other reflections evoke the 'egwugwu's exit,' Chinua Achebe's recent transition. The poet uses this passage in typical Bette-dirge fashion, to send messages to those who have gone beyond but in a critical way: the likes of Fela Anikulapo Kuti, Ken Saro-Wiwa and others. He sends the recent dead to the long dead with messages from the living: 'Greet Dele Giwa but tell of Reuben Abati/ [...] Greet Gandhi, but tell how in India/manliness is expressed in erection/ Tell too of sad Assad.'

The creator of the Frankenstein of youth restiveness and unemployment pops up in 'an encounter'; an experience familiar to many Nigerian graduates. The CEO in the poem tells the hopeful applicant with a Master's degree from proud Ibadan University: 'we have lost confidence/in Nigerian graduates./On his way out/the *maigad*, the applicant/had bantered with, said/ 'make you no mind that *yeye* man/na fake diploma him get sef/*Banza* man'. The case of one soiled finger staining the rest. Does anybody need to tell the managers of our national cakes that undernourished universities produce degrees that have lost their respect anywhere in the world, and thereby continue to fuel the time bomb?

Other poems tell of other human interests, emotions and bereavement and as it were climax in a final emptiness, anxiety and angst that befall most demiurges of culture: poets, writers and artists. The poet persona as though exhausted from the trance of the medium bewails: 'I am the empty/realization of me.' But this can hardly be said of these rich wide-ranging engravings on the rock-canvas of time. rome aboh has in this debut collection as it were taken verbal snapshots of our contemporary reality. The poems stylistically, are so pithy that, like the drama of the absurd that provides little character motivation or background story, we merely wander/wonder about the poet's real intention. But can we really circumscribe the poet or any artist's intention? 'i think,' like many of the other poems in this volume, leaves us guessing in an ever endless possibilities of art. Even though it is hasty to guess aboh's evolving style, this collection bespeaks a writer whose verse is sparse, short and pithy with statements that invite us to fill the white gaps on the pages of the book with our own thoughts in an interactive, recursive way that good writing does. The evocative lines like, 'What am I/without your cleansing wet fire?' tell of the wonder of the mystery of what he calls 'human morphology, chemistry and electricity.'

There is also an abundance of other stylistic devices like neologisms, repetitions of words and parallelisms which increase the musicality and magical quality of the words/sentences. Furthermore, the poems tend to reflect, maybe for those who are privileged to know the poet, an upbringing steeped in the classics like Greek and Renaissance literature as well as the Bible. This, however, has not taken him away from contemporary allusions that serve to paint larger pictures than what we seem to be reading before us. These pictogrammatic shots become 'lonely eyes like those of a Syrian refugee', which re-present for us the absent presence. The poems in this volume, seeming as they are rooted in the streams, hills and vales of the poet's home-village in Ohong-Obudu, provide a roller-coaster ride to some distant intellectual/mental scape which sets you thinking, uncomfortably but wizened. You cannot but savour this brew.

Liwhu Betiang, PhD.
Department of Theatre & Media Studies,
University of Calabar.

Contents

I

patriotism

Power and violence are opposites;
where one rules absolutely, the other is absent.
Violence appears where power is in jeopardy,
but if left to its own cause,
it ends in power's disappearance.

— **Hannah Arendt**

righter

Every writer
is a *righter,* Niyi Osunadre echoes.
They may write
for the gourmands in power .
They may write for the people
groaning in pain-filled penury.

As one takes this mines-ridden path
of poeticizing,
one will never tremble when hostile hooks
are thrown on one's path by self-styled messiahs;
but must tell the tales of our dying people.

Let these words soothe hurting hearts.
Let these strengthening words unhindered
stream like the Ungwu-Bedia River,
enriching the pauperized,
empowering the oppressed.

Let these words forewarn the brute.
O these words be the akpakwu*
on the tyrant's stubborn skin.
Let these words be the guilty conscience
of the king ruler.

---

* akpakwu – wild beans whose contact, especially during the dry
season, with the skin produces an awful itching.

verse

I write in verse
because I'm vexed.
And this verse must shine its rays
on these crooked paths of our vexed land.

I sing not my inherited lore
on the corridors of sycophancy;
for this verse must reach out
to the botched people of this land.

It must bear the eyes
that see the forsaken people of this land.
It must bear the ears
that listen to the wailings of torture.
It must carry the heart
that feels the sour pain
of girls caught in insane erections.

ible *

Afternoon:
a giant African rat scurrying
for hiding;
a falling
banana trunk.

Night:
Augury hooting owls,
grief-stricken mewing cats,
brutal barking dogs.

Morning:
another *politrickster* is born.

---

* ible – Bette-Bendi expression for evil omens (singular: 'uble').

hour of truth

Never again will our story go
without a proper telling
        Niyi Osundare, *The Word Is an Egg*

You can write
if you so choose
about chirpy birds romancin' the silvery sky;
about blossomin' roses sendin' forth perfumes
from virgin nectars;
about mornin' dew weavin' hands
with bloomin' frangipanis;
about fabulous fireflies dartin'
through wet evenin' grasses;
about rambunctious moths flutterin'
to the lustre of your laughter;
your enticin' laughter caressin'
her honey drippin' lips;
about blazin' rainbow
on her cloudy cheeks;
about sloshin' waterfall
at Agbokim.

All I care is to
write not in beaded words;
but in words encrusted with bitter memories,
memories of hunger-swollen-belly kids trudgin'
mine-ridden streets of Khartoum, Kabul
Timbuktu, Damascus, Maiduguri.

I will write of American drones in Karachi and Somalia.
I will write of frenzied shootings in American schools.
I will write of joblessness and corruption.

I will write of designed kidnappin'.
I will write of neglected ashibiti*
recordin' many more deaths.
I will write of workers' taxes
oilin' barren political ambitions.
I am writing of a forest *Sambisaing*
our girls; O our dear girls!

---

* Ashibiti – Bette-Bendi word for hospital

a torrent of terror

Yours is the brewing anarchy
at Tehran, Pyongyang.

Yours is the steaming jihad
in Darfur, Bamako.

Yours is the state-managed pogrom
in Aleppo, in you is the personification
of tyranny;
your torrent of sarin gas
has made many men childless,
and so will your children be fatherless
among men.

Your reign is a torrent
of inmates in Guantanamo Bay;
extricating men from women,
women from children and
children wandering like stray dogs
into the open arms of militias.

Yours is the thirty-year tenancy
in Harare: demagogic land distribution
raining hunger.

Yours, the *Putin* rush
of weapons to Syria, now Ukraine
finding solace in others' death.

Yours is the shortest, wildest
torrent of dementia:
national pardons,
pilfering petrodollars, and
a rapacious parliament
edging my unsuspecting people
to the brink of obliteration.

moment of despair

Their umbilical cords uprooted and
dumped at The Hague,

Now Bakassians* go as would refugees
without their gods,
without a home,
with annihilated yesterdays;
and beleaguered tomorrows.
Kpash!* They go without
the libation of their fishing feet.
Their loving brows no more caressed
by the morning dew.
And their ghosts like Hamlet's
wander still on that Peninsula.

O you peace-loving terrorist
Of Udi, Zaki Biam
have rendered many homeless;
your generation shall also be homeless
in the land of the living.

We thought you would have learned
from Japan at Yasukuni Shrine;
from Britain even at Argentina;
Israel at Gaza.
Now we all can attest
to the fullness
of your emptiness,
the magnitude of wickedness.

---

* Bakassians – the poet's coinage for the Bakassi people
* Kpash – Bette-Bendi exclamation word

a letter to the mp

Dear MP,
When you cajoled us to vote for you,
was the last time we saw you.
Abandon the impotent words–acrobatic
in NASS.
Come and see our matchbox houses
cramming us in on bedbugs-infested mats.
Come and see our eczema-coated skin, our only linen.
Come and see our children kwashiorkored bellies
and mumps-fattened jaws.
Come and see rodents and reptiles besieging our hospitals,
and bats ambushing our dilapidated classrooms.

To you we cast our votes,
to you have we turned.
The dog does not eat its kind.

We will leave this place for you.
You will inherit our corpses.

Whether you heed to this call or not
someday, in a balance of equation,
we all will be l
                o
                w
                e
                r
                e
                d
only to ascend before the Judgment throne,
rendering thieving accounts.

silent echoes

We can hear the silent whisper
of our own cries from hurting hearts,
as your torturous words sting and cripple
our hypertensive hearts, O *Sinator*.

Let us yet echo silently
of how to your famous wall of greed
you have nailed our undaunted aspirations.

Let us yet echo silently
of how your debilitating stay hangs
like a dark cloud over our beleaguered vision.

Let us yet echo silently
of how we are your menstrual cloth.

Let us yet echo silently in grieving pains
how you are a good component of a bad character.

if again ...

If again they come lamenting
of owning no shoes,
we will for them build a shoe factory.

If again they come weeping
of subsidies, we will tell them to remove
the subsidy on the air we breathe.

Of all the promises of fresh breathable air;
here we are, stranded
in the wildernesses of expectations.

Of all the promises of megawatts light
deep darkness torments still
our sorrow-filled-*demon-crazy* days.

Yet, our listening lobes are jarred
by sycophants' insane praise
of their impotent second coming.

Bisimillah! We voted for them
and now our leukaemia blood irrigates this land;
our foolishness for casting our votes their direction.

the blind lead the sighted

It is an impenetrable darkness:
a myopia of oblique tomorrows;
here, the real Bermuda Triangle.

Here:
the blind lead the sighted,
riches sit on wretches.
Hermes masks their faces with laughter.
We sweat to reclaim this wasting land,
they perspire from lifting *Ghana-Must-Gos.*
Our love for this land is steadfast,
their love for this land is
signified in their swelling Swiss accounts.
We yawn of haunting hunger,
they belch from excess food.
We march miles wanting transportation,
they run miles to burn out accumulated calories.
We suffer from low BP,
they die from high BP.
We perish for lack of cholesterol,
they wrestle to survive excess cholesterol.

Here:
even the tender
leaf of cocoyam is become a blade
that leaves us with merciless cuts;
what a bad season!

these dark days

"Our democracy remains robust, alive and well."
Tufiakwa!*
What they lack in intelligence,
they make up in fabricated tales.

Where do we go
from festering lies
assailing our sensibilities;
from legislators devouring
national vault even before approval;
from *pantomime dames*;
from minority becoming majority;
from mace becoming a weapon;
from glorification of shame?

As this fraudulent politics increasingly
makes us less human,
we are unconsciously conscious of
our slow march to eternal damnation.

Where do we go
from these dark days
of sorrow-packed existence?
Should we go to Endor
for Samuel's spirit to tell
where the acidic torrent first beat us?

---

* Tufiakwa – an Igbo exclamation that rejects something awful/
  disgusting.

evidences from okija

Having sold our souls
to tenders of Okija and then Soka,
they swore with maniacal pomposity:
"it's do-or-die."
They swore with zealotry:
"we will reign for sixty years to come."

As these offspring of Okija
assault our listening lobes
with fabricated, democratized vocabularies:
7-point agenda, vision 20-20-20, reformation agenda,
we are on top
of the situation,
BH offers them amnesty,
leads them into Sambisa;
and pain-packed laughter knocks us naughty.

As we die each passing day
from sneering insecurity,
from hypertension inducing sirens,
from burden of un-subsidized fuel;
awaiting our final l
          o
          w
          e
          r
          i
          n
          g,
still Sambisa births more
self-styled messiahs with oversized ego
and bloated penchant

for wealth,
for power,
for seventy virgins.

And as this once-up-on-a-time
honeyed-milk flowing land is
mortgaged to tenders of Okija, Soka and Sambisa,
and the yet to be discovered evil forests,
the cataract to tomorrow and beyond
thickens even much more.

echoes from the hills

We fear you not, Medusa.
No farmer has for the
fear of the baboon ever
planted their maize in the house.

We will echo yet aloud
from these high hills
to the ends of this spherical earth;
for this much is true:
we bartered our votes for
the science of your badness.

bystanders

We heard clattering echoes of rigged elections.
We saw them grip menacingly
to power like a suicide bomber to a location.

We saw husbands and fathers
cling to machetes and sling rifles.

And with no intent to provoke
we asked if they were headed for Afghanistan.

Shamelessly and with triumphant exuberance,
they exposed:
to Abuja, for the spoil, we go.

O, our eyes
saw our ears.

i see ...

As stubborn, sad Assad
still strays in Syria,
women have become circumstantial widows
at the prime of marriage;
and as men's third leg stares lifelessly
at their women's wet vault;
as children increasingly become fatherless;
as teenage girls absorb frustration-filled erections;
as melodious rhythm goes without
tapping feet and nodding heads;
as the Muezzin's solemn voice goes unheeded
by garrison men;
I see nothing,
absolutely nothing
but torrential rain of Russia-made chemicals
falling belligerently on Hums, Aleppo, Quasar ....

contraption

We are caught here
in this land we love
with the whole of our hearts
between the ass-kicking *militeria*
and the web of honey-coated-tongue *polithiefians.*

Going forward is as
difficult as making a U-turn.

O Jehovah, let them
we pray,
go to the baobab tree where they belong;
for their continuous stay here
has left us in extreme deliriums.

aljazeera

O Doha caster,
will you cast to the world
the fear-stricken minds,
the bomb-dazed gazes
of Easterners or
inflate the deepening divide
between the Crescent and Star
and the Cross;
Sunnis and Shiites?

Will you dig out that
ticking bomb that sits delicately
between Tel Aviv and Ramallah
or ably amplify
the hate that stares
at Tel Aviv and Tehran?

the real road

My head is a vast kingdom
Pregnant with revolutions
            Joe Ushie, *A Reign of Locusts*

This is the real road
not taken:
paying deafening silence
to stinking drainages;
to cramming in hostels;
to deepening darkness;
to empty water tanks;
to manicured late registration fees;
to indigenization politics;
to repressive grips of oppressors.

Is this the real road to graduation
in these universities?
Is applauding tormenters' madness
the real road to our peoplehood?

a wondering mind

I wonder what you would do
if the plane you were to board
was to be flown
by an inexperienced Federal Character.

I cannot help but wonder what would happen
if oil wells of the south shifted
to the east,
to the west,
to the north.

I will continue to wonder
what would have happened
if apples were never grown.

I wonder what would happen
if you were the kidnapped.

And I wonder too
if we were ruled by mindless occults.

... in our neighbourhood

Though the ATM in our neighbourhood
dispenses torn and fake naira notes
and we wonder where to
hide our hard-earned naira;

though the judge in our neighbourhood
dispenses justice to naira-lined pockets;
and the lawyer
is become a liar;

though in our neighbourhood
corruption is become their Achilles' heel;
and the police
aim their rifles menacingly at our ₦50,
as our borders leak like uninm*;

though the preacher in our neighbourhood
preaches seed-sowing in naira,
and anoints the barren with his third leg;

though the nurse in our neighbourhood
is become a merchant of babies,
and the orphanage a trafficking conduit;

though the poet in our neighbourhood
poeticizes on the corridors of economic power;

though the governors forum in our neighbourhood
is metamorphosed to a gang of gourmands;
propaganda the identity of our political ideology;
and fraud of "godfatherism" the
political template of our national modus operandi;

though we will never take to violence,
we will yet echo it from this hilltop

that there are in our neighbourhood
many more modest neighbours
who care less about lining their
generations' lives with republic's naira.

---

* Uninm – Bette-Bendi word for perforated clay-pot that cannot hold
  water for a second

smart samaritan

MTN, bank mender
we received the free-call airtime.
However, when day breaks,
we will fathom
the reason for your
unusual kindness.

II

patterns of love

God stands winding His lonely horn,
And time and the world are ever in flight:
And love is less kind than the grey twilight,
And hope is less dear than the dew of the morn.

— William Butler Yeats

labour of love

Your absence stabs me
and I die every day
waiting for you
in the cadences
of long-suffering love.

But remember that
it is an evil omen
when for too long
a snail leaves its shell.

the texan wine lover

She loved fireflies
because their fire dance
reminded her of far away Abilene.

I know about fireflies
because in Bette-Bendi a sensuous
firefly dance over your head,
foretells you will very soon marry.

This Abilene girl
painted white the streets of my hilly home.

But it was in the
tranquil atmosphere of Unibadan
that we met.

Our distinct white and black upbringing
imprisoned, we mingled endlessly:
she white, I black.
We lived and loved,
no one *colour* outshining
no one *colour* staining
the other.

I never told you, MHS
how those evenings spent between wine
defined the contours and substance of my existence.

stay here

Like dripping leaves after a torrential rainfall;
like a gazelle on a grassland;
like some Olympian-footed Ajunwa;
like the dancing vapour of petroleum in the sun;
you fizzled out.

Stay, for since I met you,
you have been going

O, you must not go elsewhere.
Stay here!
For the goat that breaks clay-pots,
does it everywhere it goes.

a sick minstrel

Let him sing
of how she occupies
the softest part of his heart.

Let him dance
to the cadenzas
of her voice.

Let him sing
of how she is the eternal
light that condemns his darkness.

Let him sing
of how his burden
she bears.

Let him sing
of how she is the stream
that snakes through his desert.

Let him sing
of how his
Red Sea she parts.

soothing laughter

He could hear them
both far and near:
rustic but soothing laughters
and melodious music
bursting forth from her lungs.
And his soul could have
never been that merrier;
his feet caught some rhythm,
and there was nothing he
could do but to dance.

For the child gets really affectionate
with those who, with lullabies,
rock it to sleep.

one moment

One moment that spelled out
to me the electricity
of our human morphology:
an incomprehensible syntax
when two separate clauses
merged into an inseparable sentence

What am I
without your cleansing wet fire?

we each saw

the twinkling sparkles,
the warm glow that passed between us
each time our eyes caught each other's.
We each felt the Tsunami-like
wave of affection criss-crossing between us
but, we each had where our hearts were.
Yet, between us there persisted some
infinite liking, a loving undefined.

And those whom we each loved and
thought loved us barricaded us
unlimitedly from taking those sparkling moments.
As though our irresponsiveness was not enough,
distance came and tore us apart the more,
drifted us across continents.

Again and again and again
those we each thought loved us
hurt us deeply.
Yet, we loved them without wavering,
and they kept at it,
hurting us as with intensity.

Each time we each felt we had held one,
from both of our hands they slipped off
as would cat fish in murky water.
Oh, we patched here, it leaked there.
Today, we are *so alone*;
needing, wanting in this cold world …

allegiance

She said it from deep places
that she will be there for him
when his contours wrinkle
and his hair grey.

She said she will hold onto him
as lightning to thunder;
as a suckling to milk-sodden nipples;
as Major Okigbo to Biafra;
as a moth to light;
as Mandela to Freedom;
as moon to night;
as Macbeth to Duncan's crown;
as Samson to Delilah;
as a preacher to the pulpit;
as an Electra to her father;
as a teacher to students;
as pollens to the stigma;
as a foetus to an umbilical cord;
as Joseph to Potiphar;
as a book to a shelf;
as a snail to its shell;
as a lost sheep to Christ.

She is one who offers
her arms when he
only asked for a hand.

warm thoughts

I hug myself
in the warm thoughts
of you.

And there is nothing greater than this:
the more I think of you,
the more saturated am I
in the warmth of your unending love.

every day

Every day I walk this path
I see you alone
smiling in the crowd;
wiping lonely tears alone
on a long face.
Come to me, dear heart,
for we two can never be lonesome.

Come,
your time has come
let me lead you away
from these self-reverential people
to where your audience lies;
to where your dignity lies;
to strip you of every garment
you wore in disguise.

I will be patient with you
for you have been so lonely
you could die …

will you?

will you stroke these glistening hairs
when they grey
will you cuddle this smoothened skin
when it wrinkles

will you kiss again and again these sparkling teeth
when age encrusts them with green

will you inhale this arresting breath
when the stench of old odours it

will you, dear?

a walk in the moon

To every night is a moon.
Their hands clung onto
each other's loosely firm.
He talked from deep places
but her eyes were watching
the moving moon.
Could this be my moon?
She let her mind ponder.

The moon's rays pierced
through shady trees; leaving
patches on the road,
revealing patches of love
laced with anxiety, anxiety
of a heart too broken.

there was another ...

you told me sometime ago
that you loved me
and i believed with the whole of my heart

i thought in you i found a friend
but with manicured lies you led me
in to the dark and abandoned me there
and when you came back
you were clad with fresh lies
yet my love for you was unfaltering

there was another when
you were loving me

i lost my mind 'cause i met you
you will not remember 'cause
you ate the flesh and i, the bone

how you stole my green innocence
how you trampled on my white rose
how i die every day waiting for
you to ever be human

III

reflections

Reflection is an active process of witnessing one's own experience in order to take a closer look at it, sometimes to direct attention to it briefly, but often to explore it in greater depth.

Anonymous

time

O time, silent recorder of events;
secret re-collector of actions;
graphic reflector of deeds;
forgetting not an iota,
remembering every bit,
even ominously.

me

Flipping through these pages
of my existence,
I see some figures
towering highest: you.

Me, an objective first
person personal pronoun,
is empty without you:
you and circumstances,
good and bad
make Me.

broken lines

Yet to the world have they spilled
tales of how he broke their hearts.

First, she was that slender
strongly instinctual beauty
in whom he was well-pleased.
Her thick-dark-manicured eye lashes,
resting over a fair-complexioned-oval face
imprisoned his oculomotor nerves
while the affair lasted.
"But she was a miscellany of temper!"
He raised his voice.

Second, she was that gorgeous gazelle on a grassland
with an Aristocratic gait.
She was astoundingly eloquent and
could talk Macbeth from sparing Macduff's Tree.
But her lips were littered
with terminological inexactitude.

Now some chronology has he lost.
"I hate chronology," he lamented.
O she was the one
who stirred in him the academic gift.
She was the *taliswoman* who shed
her incandescent rays on his crooked paths.
As desire ascended a crescendo,
she vanished into the labyrinth
of culture-religious differentiations.
She yet remains that
coin lost in a crab's hole.

And she was that academic life
companion his search rested on.

Her dimpled smiles could render Medusa's stare infertile.
But in those dimpled smiles were daggers.
In her, the chemistry of wickedness was comprehensible:
the Brutus at the Capitol;
fervent in hypocrisy.

Now he is sending these b-r-o-k-e-n lines
of his heart to all those
who mangled it.

photographs

As this flame, enkindled by
these vexed fingers of mine,
rages hungrily like wildfire during dreadful
harmattan over your photographs
taken when religion
and distance were ingredients
that spiced our luminescent love
not the reasons for our
pain-filled parting,
I well remember your
white-spot-free face like the dove of peace,
your little lonely eyes
like those of a Syrian refugee
darting from one Black face
to no Black face
in particular
in Room 71;
the cursed day my
tender heart as tenderized as
the palms of a suckling
was enrolled for breaking.

And as these photographs become ashes,
may the winds of remembrance blow
them to wherever you are
that my wrecked heart may mend
and love again.

i am ... i

that unconsumed bush on fire.
My table is set before my enemies.
I till rocks for yam mounds,
and climb the cotton tree with bare hands.
I'm he whose version of the story is never listened to,
the chewing-stick in everyone's mouth;
the very one whose obsequies
are announced before his death.
My urine turns into a stream,
and faeces make a mountain.
My in-laws ask for ants' urine
for their daughter's bride-price,
and my wife abandons me
at the middle of every wet night.
My mother died before I was conceived,
an orphan to many mothers.
I'm the frog whose gift sits
at the top of an iroko,
yet my share of meat is picked
from the midst of driver ants.

I'm dry meat that fills the mouth;
the vetch growing amidst cacti.

I am the Cassandra of the new age.

harmattan again

I can see leaves turning orange;
feel the breeze getting cooler;
hear the gentle sigh of wind in the grass.
Ah! Harmattan is creeping in poco a poco,
and I well remember me
clad in multiple rags
as my teeth rattled and clattered
in alliteration to the biting-harmattan cold.

And I am that brown dusty-footed infant
wending the winding way
to the farms at Akorgiagba.*

I more remember the fire-prone harmattan bush
sparking swiftly to the infancy
of my matches.

And the scurrying squirrels and petrified rats
O Unim-Akorgiagba* too scurried everlastingly.

Now the impotent soil stares
bare at me.

---

* Akorgiagba – very fertile farmland in the poet's hometown where
  the god of fertility lived. In time past, no one stole there and went
  unpunished by the god.
* Unim -korgiagba – the god of Akorgiagba

candle in the dark

(*for M.T. Lamidi*)

As I wend my way back
through these discordant diversities:
tongues and cultures and peoples
and religions and topographies and climates
to the hills where underneath a coconut tree
lies my umbilical cord;
I well remember Bodija market in the rain;
I remember too the Ibadan fire-catching-
and-clothes-tearing buses,
and their *were** swearing drivers.

I remember the First and the Best.
And the sweet-sad thought of leaving you
– 9 Saunders Road –
hits me with the trick of nosophobia.

And I remember even better
ascending and descending those
syntactic steps to-ing-and-fro-ing Room 601.
I remember your quick-intelligent eyes
darting through the pages of my thesis,
falling still hard
on the "non-syntactic argumentations"
and aberrant constructions.
Yet, a soothing smile massaged your brows
on that argument convincing,
on that paragraph strengthened out.
In your presence my weakness saw strength.

Like the perfect star to the men
from the East
you flickered steadily and

burnt silently and deeply and
illuminated my dark academic paths.

---

dad, and dads

Even as political quakes force us to
cringe like cornered cattle,
always we will remember you.

Of all the fatherly sacrifices you ever made,
we very well remember
your emptying your salary
into our extravagant pockets;
impressing in our hearts
we owe the same to our generation.

But this age of ours we fear:
so strangely immersed
in the lethargic thrills of the age;
doing nothing,
expecting everything.
Can we ever be like you, Dad?
Laying your life for ours ...

Of all we are today:
sunniest and coldest climes we have trod;
impressive feats we have attained;
daunting heights we have climbed;
warmest and coldest embraces we have entered;
we owe to your scolding and cuddling.

But, Dad, there are other dads;
far and near in blood:
men whose arms opened widely to us
in more ways than one;
men who taught us the
art of catching fish;
men who closed their eyes to our foolishness

and saw the Joshua in us;
men who taught us integrity;
men who taught us the dignity of work;
men who etched in our mind the power of family;
men whose exemplary paths led us to Jesus.

forgettin'

I've been romanticizing with the idea
like bees over blooming frangipanis
to write you this repenting, lovely lines.

I've busied myself seeking love,
forgettin' only you love me this way.

I've troubled myself writin' poems for those girls,
forgettin' you are Muse;
forgettin' you are like poetry written
by the fireside durin' harmattan.

I've been tangled in webs of verse,
forgettin' your melodious lullaby lured me to sleep.
I've been window-shoppin' for beautiful roses,
forgettin' you are the breathtakin' black beauty
of the hills.

I've been in the pursuit of a new life,
forgettin' you gave me life.
I've been searchin' for Arabian perfumes,
forgettin' you tied me and my faeces-stinkin'
napkin on your bare back.

I've been on the mad chase for degrees,
forgettin' you are my prime professor,
Scholar One, Professor Emeriti, home teacher…

Today, let these lines coated
with gratitude words cannot lift
shun all those manicured barriers
and reach you in the hills
like those soothing lullabies you
lined my life with
Sweet mama, O my sweet loving mama.

egwugwu's exit

Egwugwu, your passing to
the Old Silence came to us
like the coming of
There Was a Country:
mixed responses.

Surely, things have fallen apart.
The elected no longer listen to the electors.
We are exposed to acidic torrents.

Yet, we well remember
your tender tendering of
the tendrils of our literatures.

When you get to the ancestral land,
greet Fela, the lone singer of truth.
Greet Saro-Wiwa and his other patriots
slaughtered on the altar of resource control.
Tell Abacha – if you ever see him –
to come for his kinds he left behind.
Greet Dele Giwa but tell of Reuben Abati.
Greet Gani, but also tell of the comatose judiciary.
Greet the gallant Majors of our yesteryear:
Nzeogwu and Orkar
but tell of the *haramed* arm-selling Generals.
Greet Enahoro for the Independence bill,
but do not forget to say
dogs now eat their kinds.
Greet Ola Rotimi, but tell of
rain washing leopards' spot,
and cattle swallowing pebbles.
Greet Gandhi, but tell how in India
manliness is expressed in erection.

Tell too of sad Assad.

Neither the evil forest nor the sapped economy
but our bleeding hearts receive your remains
Adieu, Chinua, orphan of many mothers ....

23 May, 2013

i think

At times you need
to blow loud your trumpet.
But when the trumpeters emerge,
the sweetest tone
will be known.

At times you need
to dance on the streets
without a drummer.
But when the drummers
begin to throb their drums
the real dancers
will be known.

an encounter

In their order of award,
he painstakingly put his certificates together
and presented them to
the bulldog-like CEO.

Like an escritoire owed
several months' salary,
he sped through them degradingly

and stared ominously at the
hunger-beaten applicant whose
white shirt, by overuse,
had turned brown;
and colourful ignorance fled from
his unbridled tongue:
with a master's degree from UI
we could give you a try.
You see, the words fell from his
lips like some co-wives caught in verbal duel,
we have lost confidence
in Nigerian graduates.

On his way out,
the *maigad*, the applicant
had bantered with, said
"make you no mind that yeye man
na fake diploma him get sef.
Banza man!"

some passing
(*for Richard Abantelhe Ukwu*)

Today I am minus one cousin:

Like a short-lived dry season breeze;
like the tender freshness of sprouting
April grass;
like green ugu* leaves by the streamside
during teeth-clattering harmattan;
you rode too swiftly on the wings
of death;
leaving behind an empty scar on our hearts;
we were yet to wipe mournful tears
when the reaper's sickle cut Aboh.
Aye Unim Ada!

Though several years since your
brief, pain-filled passing,
loudly can we still hear
the echoes of your heart-warming laughter.

You live in the fertile ground of our hearts.
You live more in the memory of my verse.
Adieu, Abantelhe.

18 August, 2001

---

* Ugu – Pumpkin leaves

some encounter

His broad friendly smile pulled me
expectedly towards him.
I could have seen the grinning face
from before, the thought flickered
through my mind.

I love your lips: *Succulent.*
You have got some hips,
the words tumbled from his
cigarette-darkened lips
like water over some steep
rock in Ungwu-Bedia River
whose lapping return-call
echoes eternally in my ear drum.
He winked at me
with calculated overtures.

Will this *same* man really be *interested*
in me for fourteen years?

i am ... ii

I am the hand to hold
not to trust;
the voice to hear
not to believe

Truly,
I am the wanderer
coming and going
as they please

Quietly,
I am the mop
mopping their grime

Silently,
I am the needed road
they walk with hesitations

Ah!
I am the ear to coo into
not to listen to

I am the empty
realization of me

Kraftgriots

Also in the series (POETRY) *continued*

Joe Ushie: *A Reign of Locusts* (2004)
Paulina Mabayoje: *The Colours of Sunset* (2004)
Segun Adekoya: *Guinea Bites and Sahel Blues* (2004)
Ebi Yeibo: *Maiden Lines* (2004)
Barine Ngaage: *Rhythms of Crisis* (2004)
Funso Aiyejina: *I,The Supreme & Other Poems* (2004)
'Lere Oladitan: *Boolekaja: Lagos Poems 1* (2005)
Seyi Adigun: *Bard on the Shore* (2005)
Famous Dakolo: *A Letter to Flora* (2005)
Olawale Durojaiye: *An African Night* (2005)
G. 'Ebinyo Ogbowei: *let the honey run & other poems* (2005)
Joe Ushie: *Popular Stand & Other Poems* (2005)
Gbemisola Adeoti: *Naked Soles* (2005)
Aj. Dagga Tolar: *This Country is not a Poem* (2005)
Tunde Adeniran: *Labyrinthine Ways* (2006)
Sophia Obi: *Tears in a Basket* (2006)
Tonyo Biriabebe: *Undercurrents* (2006)
Ademola O. Dasylva: *Songs of Odamolugbe* (2006), winner, 2006 ANA/Cadbury
    poetry prize
George Ehusani: *Flames of Truth* (2006)
Abubakar Gimba: *This Land of Ours* (2006)
G. 'Ebinyo Ogbowei: *the heedless ballot box* (2006)
Hyginus Ekwuazi: *Love Apart* (2006), winner, 2007 ANA/NDDC Gabriel Okara
    poetry prize and winner, 2007 ANA/Cadbury poetry prize
Abubakar Gimba: *Inner Rumblings* (2006)
Albert Otto: *Letters from the Earth* (2007)
Aj. Dagga Tolar: *Darkwaters Drunkard* (2007)
Idris Okpanachi: *The Eaters of the Living* (2007), winner, 2008 ANA/Cadbury
    poetry prize
Tubal-Cain: *Mystery in Our Stream* (2007), winner, 2006 ANA/NDDC Gabriel
    Okara poetry prize
John Iwuh: *Ashes & Daydreams* (2007)
Sola Owonibi: *Chants to the Ancestors* (2007)
Adewale Aderinale: *The Authentic* (2007)
Ebi Yeibo: *The Forbidden Tongue* (2007)
Doutimi Kpakiama: *Salute to our Mangrove Giants* (2008)
Halima M. Usman: *Spellbound* (2008)
Hyginus Ekwuazi: *Dawn Into Moonlight: All Around Me Dawning* (2008), winner,
    2008 ANA/NDDC Gabriel Okara poetry prize
Ismail Bala Garba & Abdullahi Ismaila (eds.): *Pyramids: An Anthology of Poems
    from Northern Nigeria* (2008)
Denja Abdullahi: *Abuja Nunyi (This is Abuja)* (2008)
Japhet Adeneye: *Poems for Teenagers* (2008)

Seyi Hodonu: *A Tale of Two in Time (Letters to Susan)* (2008)
Ibukun Babarinde: *Running Splash of Rust and Gold* (2008)
Chris Ngozi Nkoro: *Trails of a Distance* (2008)
Tunde Adeniran: *Beyond Finalities* (2008)
Abba Abdulkareem: *A Bard's Balderdash* (2008)
Ifeanyi D. Ogbonnaya: *... And Pigs Shall Become House Cleaners* (2008)
Ebinyo Ogbowei: *the town crier's song* (2009)
Ebinyo Ogbowei: *song of a dying river* (2009)
Sophia Obi-Apoko: *Floating Snags* (2009)
Akachi Adimora-Ezeigbo: *Heart Songs* (2009), winner, 2009 ANA/Cadbury poetry prize
Hyginus Ekwuazi: *The Monkey's Eyes* (2009)
Seyi Adigun: *Prayer for the Mwalimu* (2009)
Faith A. Brown: *Endless Season* (2009)
B.M. Dzukogi: *Midnight Lamp* (2009)
B.M. Dzukogi: *These Last Tears* (2009)
Chimezie Ezechukwu: *The Nightingale* (2009)
Ummi Kaltume Abdullahi: *Tiny Fingers* (2009)
Ismaila Bala & Ahmed Maiwada (eds.): *Fireflies: An Anthology of New Nigerian Poetry* (2009)
Eugenia Abu: *Don't Look at Me Like That* (2009)
Data Osa Don-Pedro: *You Are Gold and Other Poems* (2009)
Sam Omatseye: *Mandela's Bones and Other Poems* (2009)
Sam Omatseye: *Dear Baby Ramatu* (2009)
C.O. Iyimoga: *Fragments in the Air* (2010)
Bose Ayeni-Tsevende: *Streams* (2010)
Seyi Hodonu: *Songs from My Mother's Heart (2010)*, winner ANA/NDDC Gabriel Okara poetry prize, 2010
Akachi Adimora-Ezeigbo: *Waiting for Dawn* (2010)
Hyginus Ekwuazi: *That Other Country* (2010), winner, ANA/Cadbury poetry prize, 2010
Emmanuel Frank-Opigo: *Masks and Facades* (2010)
Tosin Otitoju: *Comrade* (2010)
Arnold Udoka: *Poems Across Borders* (2010)
Arnold Udoka: *The Gods Are So Silent & Other Poems* (2010)
Abubakar Othman: *The Passions of Cupid* (2010)
Okinba Launko: *Dream-Seeker on Divining Chain* (2010)
'kufre ekanem: *the ant eaters* (2010)
McNezer Fasehun: *Ever Had a Dear Sister* (2010)
Baba S. Umar: *A Portrait of My People* (2010)
Gimba Kakanda: *Safari Pants* (2010)
Sam Omatseye: *Lion Wind & Other Poems* (2011)
Ify Omalicha: *Now that Dreams are Born* (2011)
Karo Okokoh: *Souls of a Troubadour* (2011)
Ada Onyebuenyi, Chris Ngozi Nkoro, Ebere Chukwu (eds): *Uto Nka: An Anthology of Literature for Fresh Voices* (2011)
Mabel Osakwe: *Desert Songs of Bloom* (2011)
Pious Okoro: *Vultures of Fortune & Other Poems* (2011)

Godwin Yina: *Clouds of Sorrows* (2011)
Nnimmo Bassey: *I Will Not Dance to Your Beat* (2011)
Denja Abdullahi: *A Thousand Years of Thirst* (2011)
Enoch Ojotisa: *Commoner's Speech* (2011)
Rowland Timi Kpakiama: *Bees and Beetles* (2011)
Niyi Osundare: *Random Blues* (2011)
Lawrence Ogbo Ugwuanyi: *Let Them Not Run* (2011)
Saddiq M. Dzukogi: *Canvas* (2011)
Arnold Udoka: *Running with My Rivers* (2011)
Olusanya Bamidele: *Erased Without a Trace* (2011)
Olufolake Jegede: *Treasure Pods* (2012)
Karo Okokoh: *Songs of a Griot* (2012), winner. ANA/NDDC Gabriel Okara
     poetry prize, 2012
Musa Idris Okpanachi: *From the Margins of Paradise* (2012)
John Martins Agba: *The Fiend and Other Poems* (2012)
Sunnie Ododo: *Broken Pitchers* (2012)
'Kunmi Adeoti: *Epileptic City* (2012)
Ibiwari Ikiriko: *Oily Tears of the Delta* (2012)
Bala Dalhatu: *Moonlights* (2012)
Karo Okokoh: *Manna for the Mind* (2012)
Chika O. Agbo: *The Fury of the Gods* (2012)
Emmanuel C. S. Ojukwu: *Beneath the Sagging Roof* (2012)
Amirikpa Oyigbenu: *Cascades and Flakes* (2012)
Ebi Yeibo: *Shadows of the Setting Sun* (2012)
Chikaoha Agoha: *Shreds of Thunder* (2012)
Mark Okorie: *Terror Verses* (2012)
Clemmy Igwebike-Ossi: *Daisies in the Desert* (2012)
Idris Amali: *Back Again (At the Foothills of Greed)* (2012)
A.N. Akwanya: *Visitant on Tiptoe* (2012)
Akachi Adimora-Ezeigbo: *Dancing Masks* (2013)
Chinazo-Bertrand Okeomah: *Furnace of Passion* (2013)
g'ebinyŏ ogbowei: *marsh boy and other poems* (2013)
Ifeoma Chinwuba: *African Romance* (2013)
Remi Raji: *Sea of my Mind* (2013)
Francis Odinya: *Never Cry Again in Babylon* (2013)
Immanuel Unekwuojo Ogu: *Musings of a Pilgrim* (2013)
Khabyr Fasasi: *Tongues of Warning* (2013)
Immanuel Unekwuojo Ogu: *Musings of a Pilgrim* (2013)
Khabyr Fasasi: *Tongues of Warning* (2013)
J.C.P. Christopher: *Salient Whispers* (2014)
Ebi Yiebo: *The Fourth Masquerade* (2014)
Paul T. Liam: *Saint Sha'ade and other poems* (2014)
Joy Nwiyi: *Burning Bottom* (2014)
R. Adebayo Lawal: *Melodreams* (2014)
R. Adebayo Lawal: *Music of the Muezzin* (2014)
Idris Amali: *Efeega: War of Ants* (2014)
Samuel Onungwe: *Tantrums of a King* (2014)
Abubakar Othman: *Bloodstreams in the Desert* (2014)